Aaron,

Bible reading is
required before
every Packer game!

Happy Birthday
Sue + Mark

The Cheesehead Bible

By Art Starr

The Loon

Twice Baked Productions
307 Granby Rd. Lake Forest, IL 60045
cheeseheadbible.net

Library of Congress
Catalogue Card Number Pending

Illustrations by Pat Baker
Design and layout by Terry Baker

This book is dedicated to
those who show in rain and snow
wearing cheese proudly.

Acknowledgements

I am grateful to all those who
encouraged me to stop talking about it
and go write a book.

I thank my family and friends
whose enthusiasm put the wind under
my tired, old wings.

Finally, I owe a debt of gratitude
to the faithful cheeseheads of yesteryear
and today, for this is their story,
written by their hearts,
across time and space.

I am only a recorder of deeds.

ORDER OF THE BOOKS
of the Cheesehead Scriptures

The Book Of
CREATION

1 In the beginning God created Wisconsin.

2 Now Wisconsin proved to be formless and
   waste and a desolation. And there was
   darkness upon the surface of the earth,
   until spring.

3 And God said, "Let there be light." And the
   sun appeared, thank God.

4 And God said, "Let the earth sprout barley
   and grass and the seed of its kind." And it
   was so.

5 And God said, "Let there be knotty pines
   so as to make knotty pine paneling for the
   taverns." And it was so.

6 And God said, "Let there be buffalo and
   spotted cows and goats and sheep," And it
   was so.

7 And God said, "Let there be badgers and
   whitetail deer and black bears." And it was
   so.

8 And God said, "Let there be sky blue
   waters with muskie and walleye, mallards and
   geese and the laughing loon." And it was so.

9 And God saw that it was good.

10 Now Wisconsin was without cheese and
    there was no darkness upon the mold in the
    cheese because there was no cheese upon
    the face of the earth.

11 Seeing that there was no one to make
    the cheese, God created the people of
    Wisconsin, male and female, He created
    them. A burly people He made them.

12 And He made them just right; the man a
    hunter and a hero for woman; the woman a
    gatherer and a beloved for man.

13 He made them as opposites so that they
    might learn to love the stranger, to honor
    the other as they honored God.

14 Then the people named Wisconsin 'Sconny,'
    And the people named themselves
    'Sconnies' and 'Sconners', which means
    'people of Wisconsin.' And God saw that it
    was good.

15 Then God blessed them and God said unto
    them, "Go forth and make every cheese
    according to its kind, for I have granted
    thee dominion over the buffalo and the cow
    and the goat and the sheep, so that ye may
    gather the milk to make cheese, that ye be
    happy."

16 And so, the burly people of Wisconsin
    gathered the milk in this wise: the men milked
    the buffalo, the women milked the cows, and
    the children milked the goats and sheep.

17 Then the people of Wisconsin made every
    cheese according to its kind.

18 And behold! Sharp Cheddar and Colby,
    Montfort and Stilton, Muenster and
    Monterey Jack! And God was delighted,
    and He told them so.

19 And the people said, "Wait! There's
    more! Parmesan and Romano, Brie and
    Camembert, Mozzarella and Provolone!"
    And God saw that it was delicious.

20 Now the burly people of Wisconsin were very
    happy and they lifted their cheeses toward
    Heaven to praise God and thank Him.

21 Then they placed the cheeses upon
    their heads so that God could see His
    congregation from on High.

22 And God called his congregation
    'cheeseheads' which means 'people of
    Wisconsin who wear cheese upon their
    heads. ' And God saw that it was good.

23 And God said, "Let the sky blue waters
    bring forth the Tommy Bartlett Water-Ski

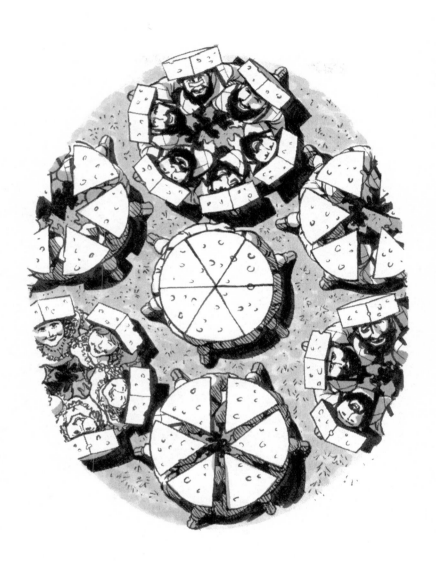

Show." And it was so.

24 And God said, "Let the waters bring forth a
    great swarm of mosquito that blackens the
    sky and bites the people." And God saw
    that it was bad.

25 Then God gave unto them screens and bug
    spray to protect them from the great swarm
    of mosquito that blackens the sky and bites
    them, for that was a sign of God's mercy.

26 And so, the people covered themselves
    in bug spray and placed screens over the
    holes they called 'windows' in the homes
    that had walls.

27 And the people rejoiced and shouted,
    "Praise be to God's mercy!"

28 And God said, "Wait! There's more!" Then
    God coached them how to plow the earth
    with the five-man blocking sled and plant the
    barley seed and harvest the barley crop to
    make the beer, which they did.

29 Whereupon the Sconnies guzzled the beer
    with much gusto. And the people were
    exceedingly happy. And God saw that it was
    almost too good.

30 Then God said, "See, I give thee footballs to
    mark the border where there be no

boundary, for I have given thee all the land of Wisconsin which is all the land between the big blue waters of lake Mich-ee-gan in the east, to the muddy waters of the river Mississippi in the west, to the big shining waters of lake Gitche Goomee up north by the Yoopers, but there be no such boundary to the south."

31 Now, when the people of Wisconsin heard God say there was no boundary to the south, the men were sorely vexed and the women worried exceedingly.

32 And they cried out, "We are sorely vexed, for there is no boundary to the south and there be no border betwixt Sconnies and outta-towners!"

33 And the people slapped their foreheads with flat stones, for they were flummoxed. And they cast their cheese hats upon the ground rejecting God's plan.

34 Then they tore their hair in despair, and prayed for deliverance to a rock in the Dells.

35 And God asked, "Why dost thou worship a rock? Was it not I who created all the rocks in the Dells? And did I not give unto thee footballs to mark the border where there be no boundary?"

36 Then the people remembered God's gift of footballs and puzzled as to their purpose no more.

37 And so, in order that His people be not vexed, God coached them to place a football centered on a virtual line stretching between the Cheddarite people to the east by lake Mich-ee-gan and the Corner Folk of the west, hard by the river Mississippi.

38 And the people did as God coached them and placed a football for a boundary marker, establishing the southern border of Wisconsin, just south of Beloit.

39 Then God coached them further and bade them mark the proper borders of all the homes, farms, and taverns of Wisconsin in like-wise fashion, for footballs were plentiful and did abide in great abundance round about.

40 And so the women gathered the footballs and the men placed the border markers as God coached them. And God saw that it was good.

41 No longer were the people vexed, for their minds were relieved to know what-was-where and what-was-whose.

42 And so the people picked up their cheese

hats and, replacing them upon their heads, begged God His forgiveness and praised God for His coaching.

43 And God said, "Now I will tell thee what-is-what and what-is-wherefore, for I give unto thee rules for living so that ye will know how to find happiness, that ye might have understanding and not fall into a state of war as is everyone against everyone."

44 And God said, "Beware, and harken unto My word, for on that day when ye dishonor My rules there will be weeping and wailing and gnashing of teeth, and the sky blue waters will turn blood red and ye will have no protection from the great swarm of evil that blackens the mind and bites the soul.

45 For on that day, ye will call evil down upon thine selves and evil thou will do unto others. On that day ye shall be accursed and think ye mocked by the laugh of the loon."

46 Then, seeing that everyone's attention had He, God said, "These rules I give unto thee as a gift, a purpose, to avoid misery, and they are these:

47 Don't get too big for thy britches.

48 Do not worship a rock in the Dells.

49 Do not call down evil under My banner.

50 Wear cheese proudly on Game Day.

51 Honor thine elders, even if ye like them not.

52 Killing people is My job, not thine.

53 Keep thy hands to thy self.

54 If it doesn't have thy name on it, it belongeth not to thee.

55 Deceiveth not in court.

56 Let not thy neighbor's stuff possess thee. For covetousness leads to envy, and envy leads to no damn good." sayeth the lord.

57 Hearing this, the multitude were in awe of God's knowledge and experience. Also, the people were in awe of the lightning bolts and thunderclaps that announced each rule.

58 For as long as the people were in awe, they were not in a state of war.

59 And God said, "No longer art thou innocent for I have told thee what-is-where and what-is-whose and what-is-what and what-is-wherefore. Now, follow My rules for living, and don't forget to enjoy Wisconsin!"

"Lightning bolts and thunderclaps
announced each rule."

60 Verily, the people loved everything that God had made, and loved God for making everything they loved.

61 And there was a great jubilation in the land and they gathered from hither and thither to celebrate God's blessings.

62 From the town of Green Bay came the meat packers, with burnt offerings of bratwurst.

63 Then dairy farmers and barley farmers came from round about with their offering of semi-soft cheeses and barley for the brewers.

64 Then came tavern owners from Milwaukee and Madison, LaCrosse and Sheboygan, Oshkosh and Fond du Lac and they rolled out the beer barrels to have a barrel of fun.

65 And so, the burly cheesehead people devoured the bratwurst and devoured the semi-soft cheeses and guzzled the beer with much gusto.

66 Then they sang beer drinking songs and did guzzle more beer and then danced the polka round about the bon-fire to the music of the oompah band.

67 And the Sconnies were exceedingly happy. And God saw that it was good.

68 Now, after his many labors, God rested and
   savored the many joys of His creation while
   He may. For, although God made people
   just right, He had given them a free will of
   their own to choose between honor and
   dishonor.

69 And He knew the Sconnies were quite
   capable of putting the sin in Wisconsin.

The Book Of
SIN

1 And it came to pass during the Octoberfest when the people were enjoying the beautiful fall foliage while guzzling beer with gusto, there arose a dispute regarding the uncertain location of a certain border.

2 For, during the night, a violent tempest had displaced the football marker such that the people could see not where to replace the ball unto its proper position showing the original what-was-whose.

3 On one side, the dairy farmer claimed it was hereabout. On the other side, the barley farmer claimed it was thereabout and they could reach agreement not, for either placement would appear to grant land at the expense of one or the other.

4 So they asked unto God how to resolve the border dispute.

5 Then God coached them to establish a line of skirmish half the way betwixt the two claims and find the true border through honorable combat, without weapons.

6 And God said, "Superior valor honors Me, thus earning its natural reward."

7 The dairy farmer asked god, "If virtuous deeds suffer loss, will not the loser of the contest think his effort in vain?" And God

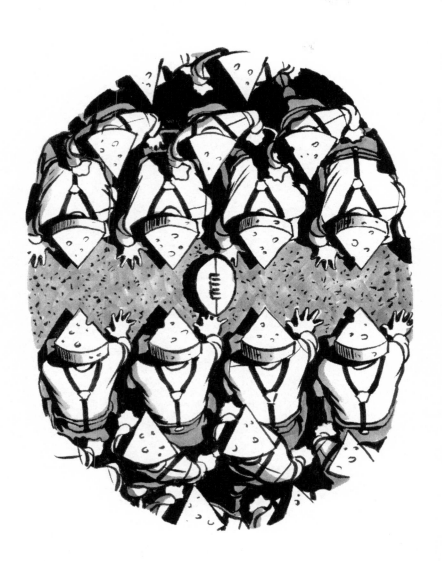

answered saying, "Honest effort honors Me also. Now, it is true that might does not make right. However, might does establish the borders."

8 And so, the people placed the football marker halfway betwixt the two claims thereby establishing a line of skirmish.

9 Then, both sides gathered together their burliest men folk round about the ball on either side of the line of skirmish, and waited for God's signal.

10 And then God said, "Ball!" And there followed a mighty collision of burly, dairy fed bodies, startling the loons, with a sound not unlike the thwack of great meaty slabs slapping the floor of the meat packing plant as though dropped from a great height.

11 And so, the tangle of burly bodies formed a great mass of mud splattered, beefy limbs struggling through the muck left by the great tempest.

12 Now the ball was slippery, not unlike the piglet in stye mud, and the struggle for possession thereof was unsure and there were many fumbles and also laterals followed by fundamentally correct tackling.

13 And the women and children, wearing

25

cheese proudly, exhorted the men to ever greater feats of courage and perseverance with shouts of encouragement, while a great chorus of quacking southbound geese passed overhead. For there was much shouting and grunting and they raised a great cacophony.

14 Now, the Lord was well pleased to witness the valor and courage of the men that he had made, for he had made them just right.

15 And he was well pleased by the loyalty and compassion of the women, for he had made them just right.

16 And God was well pleased by the valor and effort of both sides in the clash, for it honored him doubly. And nobody died.

17 One hour passed before the men, exhausted and drained of their strength, came to rest in a great heap, motionless, save for the heaving of panting chests.

18 Then the children shouted, "Again!" for they had not suffered contusions and abrasions as did those who participated in the struggle.

19 Then God declared a settlement of the border dispute - that the settling of the ball at the bottom of the monkey pile marked the

proper border. And God saw that it was fair and legal.

20 Now, the dairy farmers beheld the ground gained in the struggle and thought their victory justly won. For did not God say that superior valor earns its natural reward?

21 And they answered their own question, saying, "Fair 'n' square, dere!" So, they celebrated their superior valor and its reward. And their hearts were light for success is always easy to bear.

22 And they made a celebration to praise God and made a burnt offering of brats, boiled in beer first, put noodles on their chili and guzzled beer with gusto, boasting loudly, unaware that achievement invites animosity.

23 For the barley farmers, on the other hand, were sore and downcast, for they had lost ground in the settlement despite their valor, and they cried out to the Lord, "Did not we sacrifice in honorable battle and give honest effort, or no?"

24 And God answered, "Thine honest effort did honor Me." "Then why," they asked, "did you not honor us?" And God answered, "The Dairy farmer's glory was greater. Perhaps thou art jealous of their superior ball handling skills?"

25 Now, some of the barley farmers would not accept God's judgment and they turned away from Him for they were aggrieved and thought themselves cheated, and they no longer trusted God.

26 And so, they cast off their cheese hats and cursed God and spit upon the ground. No longer did they enjoy the beautiful fall foliage, and they heard the laugh of the loon as a mockery.

27 Now, God could not heal their wounded pride for they blocked His love with their animosity.

28 And a great swarm of evil thoughts blackened the minds of the men and the women and even the children.

29 And they said, "He is a false God that does not do our bidding."

30 And they said, "Only ourselves may be trusted to reclaim the land and reclaim justice."

31 And so the break-away barley farmers got too big for their britches, claiming mastery of their own fate. For they meant to make the world in their image and not God's.

32 Thus did they not harken unto God's word.
    Thus did they forsake God's protection.
    Thus did they not beware.

33 For they placed their faith in their own
    reason; such as the reasoning that any plan
    is better than God's plan.

34 And they reasoned further that all disputes
    are settled only when one side or the other
    was dead.

35 And so, armed with reason, they did steal
    into the dusk, securing a seclusion deep in
    the Dells.

36 There, the war party worshipped unto
    the rocks and gave thanks for their gift of
    missiles and blunt objects for to make an
    impression upon the minds of their enemies.

37 And they prayed to the trees and thanked
    them for the dangerous sharp sticks and
    pointy poles for driving home their point.

    And they prayed to the knotty pines and
38 thanked them for the bludgeons for to slap
    knots on the heads of those who disagree.

39 And, so armed, the conspirators headed
    back to the fields of contest to determine
    who is right by being the only ones left.

40 Now, the ruffians marched in close order to gain their courage. And they demonized their perceived enemy to remove the obstacle of compassion from their evil intentions, saying, "What sort of fool doth wear cheese upon their head, ain'a hey?" said one. "How 'bout I squeeze their udders?" said yet another, "Then what wouldest they say, the devils?"

41 Verily did they bear false witness against their enemy and pretended of its truth until they themselves believed the lies. After all, they thought, the stories could be true!

42 Now, as they were passing through the town of Pewaukee, the bristling mob was waylaid by the elders who puzzled over the sticks and stones and clubs, and inquired as to their purpose.

43 And their leader answered, "With these stones shall we build an altar unto God. These stakes shall we club into the ground round about the altar for a protective fence therewith."

44 Now, the elders were well pleased with their answer and commended them for their piety.

45 And the barley farmers commended themselves for their cunning deceit.

46 Now, as the self righteous army arrived
at the recently disputed border they
encountered no resistance, for the dairy
farmers, tavern owners and packers
were pre-occupied with celebrating the
Octoberfest and did not notice the evil
approaching.

47 Thinking themselves unopposed the
marauding barley farmers became
emboldened, and their leader grabbed up
the football as a possession and announced
the intentions of the mob in a loud mocking
tone, "Did God not say that He gave us all
the land of Wisconsin? Now, we have come
to claim it, and we will show you our new
valor!"

48 And they raised the weapons above their
heads, the weapons that had become their
new faith.

49 And with loud shouts and threats they
advanced upon the neighboring fields, at
first slowly, then picking up speed as the
madness swept them forward gaining ground
rapidly through the spotted cows and
the sheared sheep, scattering a gaggle of
geese, conquering ground with each step.

50 Now, the packers from Green Bay noticed
not the incursion, for they were engaged

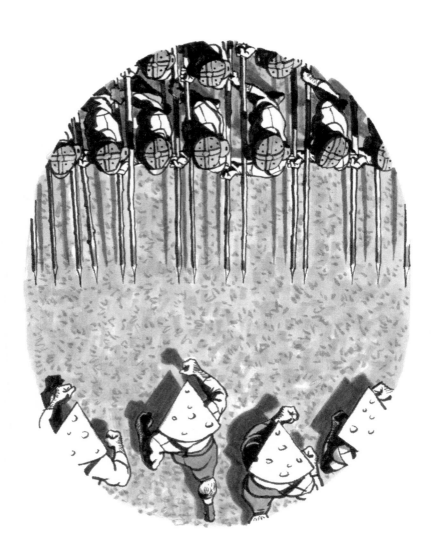

preparing a burnt offering of brats with
cheese sauce nummy in praise of God's
successful border dispute policy. And so,
the milkmaids were first to sense the danger
and alert the men folk.

51 Then, hesitating not, the brave packers
dropped their tongs and spatulas and,
unarmed, rushed headlong into the
trespassing horde, meeting them with
fundamentally sound blocking and proper
tackling technique, committing a penalty
not.

52 Just then, the sun broke through the
clouds radiating heavenly shafts of light
down upon the swelling scene, illuminating
the murderous thrust of the crazed barley
farmer's sharp weapons deep into the
flesh of the packers, their spurting blood
glistening in the sunlight.

53 And the evil doers crushed the heads of
the unarmed packers with sharp rocks and
danced, blood soaked, over the fallen,
taunting them and laughing.

54 Then did these war mongers drag the bodies
of the dead Green Bay packers to the
shore of Lake Winnebago and, with great
merriment, threw their corpses into the sky
blue waters which did turn red with their
blood.

55 And the slayers taunted the loon who did witness the murders, saying, "Where is thy laugh now, haughty loon?" For the loon was shocked into silence, and he laughed not.

56 And God asked the savage barley farmers, "Where are the packers?" And their leader replied, "Jeepers creepers, am I my packer's keeper?" And God said, "What have you done? Listen. Thy victim's blood cries out to Me from the waters."

57 Beholding this butchery were the tavern owners who, in response, rolled out the barrels and sent them careening down the hill, heavy laden with beer, accumulating great speed and weighty momentum, until several felonious barley farmers were mowed down like unto the way barley farmers mow down barley.

58 And when the tavern owners entered the field of battle, the surviving barley farmers mowed them down with the same barrels in turn. And the villains laughed, singing, "Let's have a barrel of fun!"

59 Now the barley farmers who respected God's border dispute policy bore witness to this reversal of fortune along with the dairy farmers, and together they entered the fray under a shower of rocks, and, with weapons taken from those mowed down, slew the last

of the would be conquerors without regret.
For all defensive war is just and right.

60 No longer did the people enjoy the beautiful
fall foliage. For there were weeping widows
and wailing mothers and the gnashing
of teeth of survivors across the field of
dishonor.

61 And they cried out to God, asking, "Why
is there so much sufferin' in war, eh?" And
God answered them, saying, "So that wars
will end."

62 And, as they retrieved the dead bodies of
the packers from the red blood waters, the
people complained, "Why must there be
war to begin with?" And God said, "War is
built into human nature, and can only be
abolished by abolishing humans."

63 And as they pulled the bloody stakes from
the chests of the fallen, the people pleaded
with God, "But why war?"

64 And God answered, "Does not the parent
disarm the child and impose rule? Do ye not
disarm the criminal and impose the law upon
him? Is that not a form of war? Without it,
you will have no peace."

65 And they covered the crushed heads
of the fallen with bar towels from the

taverns to hide the obscenities.

66 Now, some of the cheeseheads decided that God had made a big mistake, that He had made people all wrong. Then they threw down their cheese hats and spit upon the ground.

67 They then lectured God, saying, "We reject your creation. You have made people all wrong. So now, we must reform human nature as we reject war," said the people who went on to make perpetual war on society, for they did not realize that if God made people all wrong, then they were made wrong also.

68 Now, the faithful cheeseheads conceded that, although God made people just right, the choices people made were often wrong. And the congregation was sadder but wiser about the wisdom of deterrence.

69 And so they took an oath among themselves to arm and keep the peace, to make Wisconsin a safe place for Sconnies to follow God's plan. For they recognized that no arms is suicide, and that the abolition of arms a dangerous fantasy.

70 And so, those who rejected God and his congregation stomped off in a huff, parting ways with the faithful.

71 Now, the bodies of the slain packers were
collected and placed upon stretchers.
Then did the cheeseheads sojourn in a
great procession to the town of Green Bay,
Wisconsin to deliver the fallen heroes to
their families and observe the final rites.

The Book Of
PROMISE

1 In time, the mournful procession arrived in the town of Green Bay, Wisconsin and they laid to rest the martyred meat packers, according them full honors for their bravery and selfless sacrifice.

2 Then the congregation prayed to their Heavenly Father and invoked His spirit.

3 And God's spirit came among them, and He said unto the assembled, "Because the Green Bay packers honored Me unto the full measure, I hereby Consecrate this ground in the town of Green Bay, Wisconsin for the establishment of a Field of Honor for the celebration of valor, where war is transmuted into ritual, without weapons and without the sin of murder."

4 Hearing this, the faithful felt honored yet obligated. For the privilege of establishing a Field of Honor tasked them, and they fretted for their worthiness, for they were a small and unimportant town and modest before the Holiness of God.

5 And so they inquired as to the manner by which they should proceed.

6 And God said, "In order that ye may receive My Will for fashioning the Field of Honor, ye must, firstly, remove the snow."

"... eternal struggle..."

7 And so, the people removed the snow from the area God showed them, and they said, "Sno's sooper deep ta day, or no?" And it was hard work.

8 Then God laid out the requirements for to fashion the Field of Honor in this wise, "Know that My Laws of the Universe are above thee, like unto a gridiron for grilling, superimposed upon the sky, recording the movements of Heaven."

9 And the faithful conjured in their minds a law above men, like unto a gridiron for grilling, superimposed upon the sky, recording the movements of Heaven.

10 And God said, "Know ye that an eternal struggle between the Angels of Light and the Angels of Darkness rages across the gridiron of Heaven."

11 And the faithful imagined an eternal struggle between light and darkness raging across the gridiron of Heaven.

12 And God said, "Thusly is the earthly Field of Honor like unto the grid of Heaven."

13 And the faithful cried out, "So, the Field of Honor shall be on earth as it is in Heaven?"

14 And God said, "Yes."

15 And the faithful cried out, "So, we are like unto the Sons of Light and our opponents are like unto the Sons of Darkness, or no?"

16 And God said, "Exactly."

17 Then God declared the dimensions of the gridiron on earth, saying, "The grid shall be marked with chalk lines one half a handspan wide, forming a rectangle with a length of two hundred cubits, and a width of one hundred and six and a half cubits plus one third a handspan."

18 "This shall constitute the disputed ground wherein the skirmish proceeds, lengthwise, with the moving line of skirmish athwart the width thereof, until reaching the last ground lines at each end called goal lines." said God.

19 And the assembled laid out the ground of disputation as God commanded.

20 And God said, "There shall be, added to each end of the disputed ground, zones called 'end zones' as wide as the rectangle and measuring twenty cubits deep. These zones are for scoring with the touch down of the ball."

21 And the people laid out the end zones as God commanded.

22 Then, unto one another, they inquired,
    "Dijeet?" which means, did you eat? And
    they cried out to God, "Give us this day our
    daily lunch-break and refreshment for our
    souls."

23 Then God blew the Heavenly Noon Whistle
    and He refreshed their souls while the tired
    burly folk filled their bellies with fried cheese
    curds plus herring on crackers for good luck.

24 After lunch, God said, "At both ends of this
    gridiron, centered on each goal line, shall
    stand two posts twenty cubits tall and twelve
    handspans apart with a crossbar affixed
    between the two posts thirteen and one half
    handspans high."

25 "They shall be called 'goal posts' for they
    stand upon the goal line, and the area above
    the crossbar and in between the upright
    posts is a goal for kicks." said God.

26 Perchance, one goal post was built
    incorrectly, owing to a mistake, caused by
    the use of a large foam hand to measure
    hand spans.

27 Now, they blamed one another for to
    escape God's displeasure, saying, "Your
    upright is too long," while the others said,
    "your upright is too short, for behold, the
    crossbar touches it not!"

"... parting the players..."

And they beseeched God to lay the blame
accordingly.

28   And God said, "I will forgive thee if thee first
forgive one another, for how so can thee
ask for that which thee will not give unto
another in return?" And so they forgave
one another and then asked God to forgive
them.

29   Then God forgave them, and they built the
goal posts as God commanded.

30   Then God said, "There shall be, clothed in
stripes, judges upon the field to enforce the
Code of Honor by penalizing dishonor."

31   God said, "Judges shall stretch their hands
over the field thus parting the players upon
completion of each play."

32   And God said, "There shall be a clock to
mark the moments and limit of disputation
time, for ye are inside of time as I am outside
of time."

33   And God said, "There shall be one hour for
each contest, including a time-is-out for
resting at the halfway-time, for I am the God
of beginnings, middles and endings."

34   And so they built the clock as God
commanded.

35 God said, "There shall be a tally board, posted upon which shall be the record of score by numbers during the border disputation of touch-downs and kicks-through-goals. The tally at the end of disputation time shall determine the final reckoning of victory and defeat."

36 Then they did fashion the tally board as God instructed.

37 Then God added, "Upon the settlement of each contest ye must remove the numbers of the tally thereof, and not add them to the next contest in order to gain advantage thereby."

38 In that way did God lead them not into temptation. For He meant to protect them from evil.

39 Then God said, "Thou shalt provide to the judges an instrument with which to mark challenge and measure merit, by affixing to the bottom of two poles, each eight handspans tall, a length of chain twenty cubits long stretched between them."

40 And the faithful fashioned the instrument with which to mark challenge and measure merit.

41 Then God said, "The surface of the gridiron

shall be grass. Living, growing, actual green grass. The kind ye moweth."

42 Thusly were the shepherds commanded to lead their sheep for to do the mowing.

43 God said, "There shall be women arrayed outside the gridiron, along the sideline for safety, to prance about, wiggling and waving pompoms, exhorting the men to deeds of valor. And they shall be a delight to behold, for I created women just right."

44 Upon hearing this, the men gave out a great shout of joy and the women wiggled and squealed with delight. For the men desired to be champions for the women, and the women desired to be beloved for the men.

45 "This then," said God, "constitutes the Field of Honor. A stage for warriors, judges, and marching bands with attractive majorettes."

46 And God said, "Ye shall call each contest a 'football' game, in honor of border markers ye place at your feet when marking for boundary, and also because of the kicking and punting."

47 And God said, "Every contest shall be inaugurated by a flippeth of the coin, for every gain requires the element of chance, here's hoping at least we'll find romance!"

And they heard God give out a quiet chuckle, and God said, "Ignore that last line, just a lyric from a song I'm writing."

48 And the congregation was surprised not, for they were accustomed to God working in mysterious ways.

49 Then said the lord, "Ye shall fashion, as a system of sound, an array of horns round about the Field of Honor for announcements, and reports of lost children."

50 Now, the moment they finished installing the system of sound, God's voice came over the horns, for God was among them, and they felt His presence.

51 And God said unto them, "Harken unto My word, for I am among thee." Then God paused until the shrieking squeal of amplifier feedback subsided.

52 Then God said, "Harken unto My voice and hear My promise, for I shall bless thee and multiply thee very much, for cheeseheads will hail from all parts of the earth, including all fifty states."

53 Upon hearing this, the congregation stood agog in amazement.

54 And God said, "I will give unto thee and the small town of Green Bay, Wisconsin the most successful professional football franchise of all time."

55 Hearing this, the faithful held their breath in astonishment.

56 And God said, "Thou wilt be the owners of teams of champions by way of thine own selfless tribute, for pride of ownership and proof of faith, for a possession unto time everlasting. It will belong to thee as ye belong to Me."

57 Hearing this, the congregants were thunderstruck and fell to their knees in abject supplication.

58 And God said, "Green Bay, Wisconsin shall be exalted upon earth. For its name shall be made great, thereby earning unto it the mantel of TITLETOWN."

59 Hearing this, the faithful wept with joy.

60 And God said, "I will bless them that bless thee, and he that calls down evil upon thee I will curse, but..." then, after a very important pause, God continued, "Harken unto my word, for if ye call down evil upon YOURSELVES, I will curse thee TEN-FOLD!"

62 And the people did gasp and worry
exceedingly.

63 Lo, the congregants weighed the cost of
their faith against the blessings of God and
decided that, as a bargain, it wasn't too
awful bad.

64 Then a cheesehead asked of God, "How
shall we find these teams of champions?
Where shall we seek?"

65 And God answered, "A leader will be born
among thee, a champion, a judge of warriors
abilities, and much skill throwing the forward
pass."

66 And they pressed God, asking, "How shall
we know him?" And God answered, "He shall
be a burly man with curly hair, curly and
burly. And he will overwhelm thee, and ye
wilt be unable to resist him."

67 And God ended by saying, "Choose My
Rules For Happiness and enjoy Wisconsin!"
Then God went up from them to His
Heavenly Sky Box.

68 Now, the people were weary of body and
tired of brain, toiling in God's employment.
For they were but sinners, accustomed not
to long exposure in the presence of God.

69 And so, they made a baked offering of Menominee Falls meat balls, an offering of squeaky curds from Kenosha, then rolled out the barrels from Baraboo for to have a barrel of fun to the music of the squeeze box and the glockenspiel, round about the bon-fire.

70 And cheeseheads yodeled and laughed like unto the loon, for they were exceedingly happy.

71 Then did the people return to their homes, farms, and over-the-tavern apartments, whereabout they awaited the foretold arrival of the expected one.

The Book Of
LAMBEAU

1 Now it came to pass, in the small town of Green Bay, Wisconsin a leader of men was born, who's name was Lambeau. And the Lord blessed him, for the spirit of the Lord moved in him.

2 And he grew to be a stalwart fellow, ruddy, and handsome in appearance, with a shock of curly hair that attracted the knick-name 'Curly,' for that was what everyone called him. And he was a burly fellow.

3 Now, many were the tall tales told of Curly's prowess and deeds of valor:

4 For it was said that, as a babe, Curly changed his own diapers.

5 That once during the hunt he tackled a ten point buck and then, in a magnanimous gesture of good sportsmanship, let him go.

6 That once, upon the frozen waters of Green Bay, Curly defended his ice-fishing hole against its usurpation with a forearm shiver that Sasquatch never forgot.

7 Alas, the tall tales fell short against the true tale of Curly Lambeau.

8 Now it came to pass, Curly matriculated at the University of Notre Dame where, under the tutelage of Knute Rockne, Curly dideth

major in the study of border disputation, for he was a naturally gifted blocker, tackler, and forward passer of the ball.

9 Alas, for, unlike his classmates, no market awaited to receive his services, for no football profession obtained wherewith he might trade his skills.

10 And so, finding his destiny warming the bench, Curly returned to his small and unimportant hometown of Green Bay, Wisconsin where he traded his strength for wages at the Indian Meat Packing Company.

11 And he cried out to the Lord, "So, God, this be my destiny? Just slaughterin' bears and lions and rams and panthers and cardinals and who knows what else?"

12 And God said, "Yes."

13 Now, perchance, as old newspapers blew in the wind and wrapped about Curly's shins while he shuffled through the only alley in Green Bay, Wisconsin wearing a blood stained apron, he came upon the town-crier, who was also a devout cheesehead. And they were well met, the crier praising Curly's gridiron talents and passion for border disputation.

14 Then Curly confessed despondency over

his uncertain destiny, whereupon the town crier offered to make a tribute of his own special knowledge for the purpose of recruiting champions should Curly desire to lead them.

15 "A most generous and honorable tribute, but, alas, we have no grubstake for uniforms or equipment, for the cost is greater than you or I can pay, or no?" replied Curly, who would have played in his pajamas if they'd let him, for, like unto all Sconners, Curly did everything in his pajamas.

16 And so they said, "Meecha lader," hopeful for the future but without remedy.

17 By and by, Curly carried his troubles to the executive offices of the meat packing plant and laid his broken dreams at the feet of the owner.

18 Now, the owner beheld this curly and burly fellow with curious recognition, for he remembered the words God had spoken about the burly man with curly hair who would overwhelm them and have skill throwing the forward pass, for the owner also was a cheesehead.

19 And the owner said unto Curly, "We are the faithful and will pay tribute of grubstake unto the expected one for to realize

civilized combat upon the Field of Honor in celebration of men's valor. Are you he, the expected one?"

20 And Curly replied, "I sure wasn't expectin' that!"

21 Then the owner bid Curly await his pleasure, whilst with the officers of the plant he did huddle. Among them it was agreed that the prophecy was fulfilled by half thus requiring further proofs.

22 Then the accountant wondered aloud, "How so shall he overwhelm us, as states the prophesy, for we are many and he is one?"

23 Knowing not, the owner and officers returned to Curly and approached him in a tight, defensive bunch.

24 Then did the owner test Curly, saying, "It is important that we know of your skill throwing the forward pass."

25 Whereupon Curly arrested a large cheese from a lunch tray round about and, by an open window, threw a perfectly timed cheese pass spiraling into the basket of a passing bicyclist, who was grateful for the free cheese, two stories below.

26 Then the three witnesses nodded in agree-

ment and said, "We saw whatcha did dere," for they beheld that Curly was, indeed, the expected one, and offered unto him their tribute.

27 Then Curly, with a whoop and a rush, overwhelmed them with a burly cluster hug, lifting them off the ground and swinging them to and fro so that their legs whipped about.

28 Then, without allowing their feet to touch the floor, he carried them to the nearest tavern where, surrounded by knotty pine paneling, he spoke of many prospects round about and all their abilities and all his strategies and tactics and sneaky plays, the promise of the forward pass, and all the teams round about hankerin' for a dust up.

29 And so, the packers of Green Bay grubstaked the uniforms and equipment joyously, for they were believers, and felt honored for the privilege.

30 And to honor the tribute of the Green Bay packers, Curly named the team. . . the Indian Packing Company.

31 And it came to pass, the first season commenced and Lambeau's select few smote the unworthy from round about who had hankered for a dust up: Milwaukee's Maple

Burying the Miners of Stambaugh.

Leafs, Oshkosh's Professionals, Racine's
Iroquois, Sheboygan's Company C, and
Marinette's Northerners; shut them out
every one.

32 For no one round about could defeat
Lambeau's heroes save one, those brutes
of the borderland, the Beloit Fairies who
did smite the Packers seven to nothing, their
only defeat, which brought great shame and
ridicule upon The Indian Packing Company.

33 Now it came to pass, ownership of the meat
packing plant changed hands and changed
names to the Acme Packing Company, but
the staff changed not, for the meat packing
plant was a cheesehead stronghold.

34 Then did the new owners, in their turn, pay
tribute to civilized combat. Thus did Curly's
champions of virtue wear the name of the
Acme Packing Company.

35 Then did the Acme Packers, again, smite
the upstarts of Wisconsin, outshining the
All-Stars of Milwaukee, giving unto the
Menominee Professionals a professional
beating, blunting the tooth of The North
End Badgers of Marinette, annihilating
the Legions of KauKauna, and burying the
Miners of Stambaugh.

36 Verily, there was no one in all of Wisconsin to

Beloit Fairies.

challenge their scoring prowess or breach
their stout defenses, for all fled before
them, save one, the Beloit Fairies, who
delivered, again, the only loss suffered by
the Acme Packers that season.

37 Twas that which they spoke of not, for it did
stick in Curly's craw.

38 Now it came to pass, a new league of
football emerged which stood upon a
national stage, where, as never before, big
frogs who outgrew little ponds could go to
find larger lily pads that fit their big burly
frog butts.

39 And so, Curly offered personal tribute,
thereby gaining entrance to the league,
and the Acme Packers took their burly
bigness out of the little pond and into the
bigger pond and joined their equals, fellow
survivors of a great winnowing that would
start afresh in the League of National
Football, to establish a national hierarchy of
valor.

40 Now some teams returned each year with
name unchanged, such as Bears of Chicago,
Giants of New York and Cardinals of pretty
much everywhere.

41 Some returned named afresh; Detroit's
Wolverines, Panthers, Tigers and Lions.

42 Some did not return, such as Bulldogs of Canton, Yellow Jackets of Frankfort, Bison of Buffalo, Eskimos of Duluth, Maroons of Pottsville, and the Providence Steamrollers who ran out of steam.

43 And finally, some that never should have been, such as Yankees from New York and Dodgers from Brooklyn.

44 Now, in the bigger pond, the Acme Packers were equals on the Field of Honor earning respect, but off the field, light in the wallet, and bereft of the opportunities advantaging the filthy stinking rich ball clubs from the Massive Metropolitan Molochs with their painted women and pasty men, sky scrapers and twenty-three-skidoo, big talk and even bigger piles of money, money, money.

45 For Green Bay was but a speck upon the landscape, and poor, with room only for one slum. A subway had they not, for they were a hick town.

46 And so, the spirit of God moved the Chief of the town criers in Green Bay to gather the congregation and call them to their purpose.

47 Firstly, the Chief enlisted four other devout cheeseheads for to form an owner guardianship: the grocer, the lawyer, the

doctor, and Lambeau the packer. Together, they became known as the 'hungry five', for they were burly Sconners and enjoyed cheese exceedingly.

48 And they established a Charter under which every member of the cheesehead congregation was offered ownership by selfless tribute, without recompense, for indeed, pride of ownership and proof of faith was their most cherished reward. And, of course, to keep the team in Green Bay.

49 Thus did the congregation assume ownership of the Green Bay Packers, just as God had promised. For they were the ever faithful, cheering in rain and snow. And they wore cheese proudly.

50 Now, the Green Bay Packers waxed mighty for Curly was a tireless leader who led his heroes on the field and coached them to perfect practice daily to make perfect play on game day.

51 And so, in this way, did they slaughter the Bears, cut down the Giants, eviscerate every feline of its kind from Detroit and all the other big shot cities did they defeat in turn so that, by and by, the Green Bay Packers obtained the pinnacle of perfection and recorded the first undefeated season in the history of the big pond.

52 Curly's pride was such, he busted his vest.

53 For behold! The Green Bay Packers became Champions nay once, nay twice, but thrice! Their valor and glory unmatched against the best the nation could muster, for they sent the head bangers howling upon a flatbed to Palooka-ville.

54 And lo! Green Bay, Wisconsin, though still the smallest city in the league, was unimportant no more.

55 Verily, it was crowned with the mantel of 'TITLETOWN' by acclaim and national renown. For the people extolled the name of Curly Lambeau and the Green Bay Packers.

56 And the faithful cheeseheads beheld the glory of victory, testifying to God's promise fulfilled, the fruit of their sacrifice. And they were exceedingly happy.

57 Now, it came to pass that a great economic depression o'er came the land, and the trousers of the hobos flapped in the breeze of the passing freight trains, the women worried, and times were hard.

58 Now, the cheeseheads suffered also, but did not jump out the windows of tall buildings, gnash their teeth, or worship a rock in the Dells. Rather, they kept faith,

counted their pennies, and paid tribute dear
to God's great game.

59 Thusly did the Packers prosper while other
teams languished, perishing in the ditch hard
by the hobo camp.

60 And, behold! The Green Bay Packers, led by
Lambeau from the sideline, won three more
Championships before the end of the great
overseas war, and the fame of Curly waxed
great, and it was pleasing unto him.

61 And as his fame grew, in that way did
his pride and self regard grow, and he
fancied himself a celebrity, and forsook
the company of the common cheesehead
in favor of throwing beach ball bombs
to blonde bomb shells and tackling Miss
America in the sands of Malibu.

62 For Curly had traded TITLETOWN for
Tinsel Town, and earned yet another nick-
name, 'The Earl of Hollywood.'

63 And it was whispered that Curly had gotten
a little too big for his britches. For now, the
faithful knew him not, for he was tan, and
they were not.

64 Now, as Curly turned toward himself and
away from God, a utopian vision arrested his
attentions as he beheld the aging Rockwood

Lodge perched atop a limestone bluff,
fifteen miles up the eastern shore of the
Bay. For he imagined it could be an earthly
paradise.

65 There, he thought to build a kingdom and
rule as the 'King of Football'; a Palace
for his Royal Reign; a Regal Stable for
his Champions and Royal housing for
their families; a Royal Outhouse for his
Consecrated Constitutionals.

66 By and by, his Majesty deigned to grace the
congregation and Guardians with his lofty
presence and grandiose plans, looking sun
kissed and well rested in a colorful Hawaiian
shirt, white slacks, and two-tone shoes.

67 Curly then described his glorious
hallucination and its many delights, then
commanded the owners to empty the
treasury for to realize his vision.

68 "Art thou speaking of the old monk's retreat,
abandoned and forsaken along the upper
shore?" they asked, "The one that is a
shambles?"

69 "Tis called ... Rockwood - Lodge," said
Curly, slowly and imperiously, adding, "Tis a
Shangri-La, doncha know?"

70 Now, the owners thought Curly unmindful as

to the virtues of frugality, and, fearful for the security of the team's affairs, said unto him, "Our coffers are low and the bills go without payment. We would assume a great risk to realize your vision and maintain it also."

71 But Curly disagreed in regards to risk, for he was a warrior and cared not for concern of safety.

72 And so, indignant at their failure to satisfy his demands, Curly dismissed their apprehensions with a Royal wave of his hand, saying, "Ye of little faith," and offered his own personal resources in sacrifice to purchase the property, demonstrating his beneficence, and will.

73 In this way, the naysayers were disarmed, for Curly's offer outflanked the owners position. And so, like unto always, Curly had his way, for they could resist him not.

74 Now, the owners rationalized their consent by deferring to Curly's legacy of success, having grown dependent upon his leadership.

75 And yet, a lingering unease obtained among them regarding Curly's curious state of mind, giving unto them pause for the coming wages of their cowardice.

76 And it came to pass, owing to his blissful distraction, Curly neglected his coaching duties, thereby inviting the meddling mischief of owners, causing a downward spiral of gridiron degradation upon the Field of Honor.

77 The owners blamed Curly's distraction, yet claimed no blame for themselves, despite their complicity. And in that way turned also a blind eye to Curly's profligate spending on lavish renovations and extravagant adornment for his Castle On The Bluff.

78 And lo! The Field of Perfect Practice caused perfect suffering and injury unto his Champions. For the surface was exceedingly hard such that, among its victims, it became known as 'the rock' at Rockwood Lodge.

79 Yet, Curly dismissed their complaints as so much rabble rousing, the result of ingratitude in the face of all his Gracious Benefactions.

80 And he drove them to a distraction as great as his own until the team a wreck and the coffers bare ensuring their descent into penury.

81 Now, the diminutive town of Green Bay, Wisconsin was too small for the Green Bay Packers AND Curly Lambeau's Grand

Utopia so that the sale of Rockwood Lodge seemed the only remedy for their desperate situation.

82 Yet Curly had qualms not, for he had a plan to keep both team and utopia together. He proposed private ownership of the Green Bay Packers.

83 "Heresy!" cried the owners in perfect unison. "For is not the abolition of cheesehead ownership a repudiation of God's munificence?" asked the well read owner. "Cheesehead ownership was given by God for a possession unto time everlasting!"

84 And the congregation took up the chant, "Heresey, heresey, heresey!"

85 "It is my opinion," shouted Curly, "that what we needeth is more money and fewer cheeseheads!"

86 Whereupon, the owners upped the rhetorical ante, chanting instinctively, "More cheeseheads and more money! More cheeseheads and more money! More cheeseheads and more money!"

87 Then did the congregation vote unanimously to expand the franchise, multiplying cheeseheads and increasing tribute for to

garner more money. And Curly was undone.

88 The real owners had finally owned up to
their responsibility thus requiring Lambeau's
leadership no more.

89 Then from him they took all authority,
excepting the right of resignation, and Curly
did exercise that right.

90 And so, after thirty years and six
championships as founder, player and
coach, thirty years of organizing the faithful
and the warriors, thirty years of toil putting
TITLETOWN on the map, Curly Lambeau
parted with the owners under a cloud
of acrimony, and they went upon their
separate ways.

91 Only God knows how much it broke Curly's
heart, for Lambeau showed it not.

92 Now, the greater tribute envisioned by
the owners was an emollient for the long
term, but couldn't remedy the liability of an
unwanted and useless Shangri-La in the
short term, for no buyer could be found.

93 So that now, the owners apprehended
the loss of team in addition to the loss of
coach as the cost of their dissipation, and
began to despair, for their debt was fat and
prospects slim. They prayed for a miracle.

"... and fewer cheeseheads!"

94 And then, lo and behold, a miracle! Though
not from Heaven. For it was Hell-Fire
rose up and consumed Curly's Castle in a
demonic fire-ball that startled the loons,
destroying all.

95 And 'all' was what the owners reported
upon the insurance claim which,
miraculously, settled all team debts. And the
owners were greatly relieved, and they did
rejoice, quietly.

96 Now it came to pass, an inquiry proceeded,
to determine the inferno's cause, for its
source was a mystery.

97 The cheeseheads in the fire department
found nothing to identify.

98 The cheeseheads in the police department
found nothing to solve.

99 The cheeseheads in the prosecutors office
found nothing to indict.

100 The cheeseheads from the insurance
company found nothing to question.

101 The cheeseheads in the news rooms
reported the fire as, "More bad luck."

102 And so, the great Rockwood Lodge fire
remained, and remains, a total mystery.

103 Now, verily, there are no mysteries for God,
for God IS the mystery. A mystery that
keeps His promises.

104 And God said, "Cheeseheads, harken unto
My word, for wicked are thy ways, for ye
have called down evil upon thine selves!"
And he cursed them TEN-FOLD, as He
promised He would do.

105 And the curse that God laid upon them
lasted ten years exactly, no more, no less.

106 And so, for ten, long, insufferable years,
God's curse brought forth a great swarm of
misfortune upon The Green Bay Packers
which did bite them, for they had become
like unto a quivering morsel of ham gel.

107 Endless, agonizing seasons of ignomin-
ious defeat and abject humiliation made
unbearable by ridicule and gibes that cut
deep.

108 Now, the owners became alarmed at the
team's disgraceful descent and sought
to help by meddling in coaching affairs
beyond their ken, which made things worse,
and invited more meddling for an endless
downward cycle of failure.

109 Even the frequent changing of head
coaches helped not. For they were cursed

by God, and could not escape His
retribution.

110 Now, the congregation chafed under this
exaction for several of years before they
thought to lift the curse with an offering
of New Stadium that would honor God and
redeem their souls.

111 And so the congregation raised funds to
build New Stadium, and they did labor
exhaustingly, lifting great weights and
placing stone upon stone until, at last, they
hired professional builders to do it right.

112 And behold, it was a token worthy of their
repentance, announcing their contrition.

113 Alas and alack, the curse obtained, for no
relief did they obtain, for God had said ten
years, no more, no LESS.

114 And so it came to pass, that the curse would
not pass.

115 Lo, the Green Bay Packers suffered greatly
a plague of fumbles, bad snaps, broken
plays, whiffed punts, missed tackles, missing
teeth, and blisters that festered.

116 Their shoe laces did they affix one onto the
other in confusion, causing them downfall
and difficulty returning to an upright position.

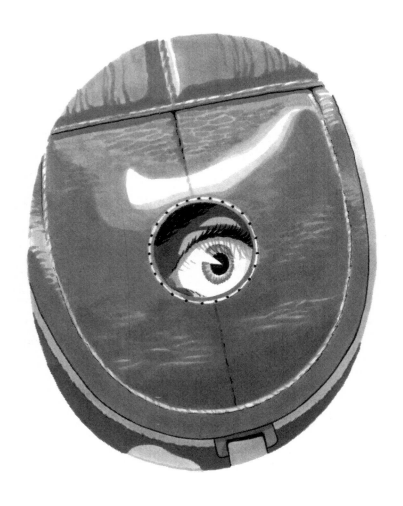

117 Their helmets became twisted about
their heads such that they beheld the
surrounding calamity by way of the ear hole.

118 For God had clouded their minds, causing
them to speak in tongues within the huddle.

119 Thusly were they brought low.

120 Now, some thought to retrieve God's
pleasure by a return to the ancient rites that
had sustained them in the past.

121 And so they made burnt offerings of
bratwurst with sauerkraut, devoured
Limburger cheese and cried out, "Lord, have
mercy upon us, for we are only Sconnies,
and we are weak, but yours is the power and
the glory forever and ever."

122 And God answered them saying, "Despair
not, for I have not forgotten thee. I will
bless thee, and send thee one who walks in
My way. A good Catholic boy who will be
a blessing unto thee, and help thee lift the
curse from your midst. Verily, he will lead
thee to glory."

The Book Of
LOMBARDI

1 And it came to pass, a man of God came among the Green Bay Packers. And his name was Vince Lombardi, who came from the good Catholic neighborhood of Sheepshead in Brooklyn, whereabout he learned to begin every day of his life in humble prayer before the altar of God.

2 Now Lombardi was a stout fellow, and his stubborn refusal to give ground proved useful upon the gridiron, and won for him acclaim, for he was an unmovable member of Fordham's celebrated offensive line that would not yield, the 'Seven Blocks of Granite.'

3 Now, upon his inaugural day as head coach of the Green Bay Packers, Vince Lombardi did, forthwith, go to Church. There did he humble himself before authority, seeking strength.

4 After Church, he entered the meeting room of players and coaches, and drove out the meddlesome owners in a brusque fashion, chasing and swatting them vigorously upon their hind quarters.

5 For he meant to protect his warriors and coaches from the well meant but misguided mischief of those who knew not regarding the study of border disputation.

6 Then Lombardi addressed the gathered
Packers and introduced his Trinity
saying, "Think ye only upon three things:
God, family, and the Green Bay Packers."
Whereupon, those who assumed they were
playing for the Cleveland Browns, left the
room.

7 Then Lombardi said, "If ye think not thou
art a winner, ye also belong here not!"
Now, be it known, the Packers did think
themselves belonging not; losers dwelling in
self loathing for their disgraceful record of
the years last. Especially during the fourth
quarters.

8 And so, hiding their shame, in their seats
they remained.

9 Forsooth, Lombardi could sense their shame
and the stupor that dideth envelope them,
deciding upon an easy question for to build
their confidence, asking, "If winning be not
important, why doth we keep score?"

10 Then, following a disturbing length of
silence, the accursed mind fog of the
Packers began to lift, and they exclaimed,
"We doth keep score for to see who is the
winner!"

11 And a great swelling of pride inflated the
room full of Packers, self satisfied with their

new found insight regarding the purpose of the game.

12 Then, Lombardi presented another poser, asking them, "If we have not the will to win, do we not defeat the purpose of the game? For does not the bear, the buck, and the ram enter the fight with the purpose of winning?" And they agreed it was natural.

13 "The way of winning is through humility before authority," he said, "God's a winner. Let's put him on our team." But the Packers understood not the way of strength through humility and bade him explain.

14 "Worry impedes action. When, humbly, we sacrifice our burden to God we proceed unencumbered, free from self concern, and worries have we not," said he. "Thus we gain freedom of action inside the discipline of authority. Thus we gain sureness of action."

15 Then Lombardi testified, "Do not the cheeseheads gain strength of ownership through selfless sacrifice? Will we not honor their sacrifice by a sacrifice of our own?"

16 And so, in this way, did Lombardi explain strength through humility and obligate them to their purpose.

17 Now the Packers did puzzle over whether a

coach or a preacher Lombardi be, and,
deciding upon the latter, nick-named him
'The Pope.'

18 And yet, despite their jests, they wondered
at his reverence, for they had never
witnessed his like before.

19 For often did he humble himself before
them; admitting his mistakes; his deference
to subordinates; never too big for his
britches, despite the barking.

20 Now, the warriors, plying a brutal trade,
could not accept less than fearless
leadership in the battles to come. And
Lombardi, it seemed to them, feared nothing
save God. And so, the Packers gave unto
Lombardi a try out.

21 Then did practice commence and Lombardi
drove his Packers without mercy; withering
wind sprints; laps around the Great Lakes;
tip-toeing in and out of tires on the ground
followed by tackling the Michelin Man;
commanding them to dance the Panamanian
Carioca for hours to build their endurance.

22 For, he said, "Fatigue maketh cowards of us
all!" And the tired cowards knew that it was
true, for the pain in their legs confessed to
the craven habits of their past.

23 Then Lombardi demanded his Packers dive onto the ground and pop back up again with never ending repetition for such a length of time as gave them to glimpse eternity.

24 And he encouraged them, saying, "Behold, to be knocked to thy knees and then coming back up, that is real Glory!" And his Packers complained of too much Glory.

25 "The good Lord gave ye a body that can stand most anything. It is thine mind ye must convince," said Vince. "The harder ye doth work, the harder it is to surrender!"

26 And so, the Packers convinced themselves that surrender to hard work just might end fourth quarter surrender.

27 Finally, exhausted and spent, they repaired to the training table, training themselves to devour prodigious amounts of food without need of coaching, excepting Lombardi's prayer of Grace before the meal.

28 By and by, the bodies of the Packers did toughen. Then did Lombardi cast down the false playbook of the past into the abyss.

29 Gone were the failed stratagems of 'first down and punt' and 'avoiding injury by avoiding contact' and 'call time out for a quarterback sneak out of the game.'

30 And Lombardi said unto them, "In their flight, do not geese share the burden of leadership equally among themselves by rotation? Let us humble ourselves before their example."

31 And so, he gave unto them a plan with fewer plays containing more chances for success in this wise: that within the purpose of every play, each player was granted freedom to counter the opponent's move in such a way as to always make the opponent's move the wrong move and his own the right move.

32 Thus did the Packers run to the daylight created by the opponents wrong move.

33 In this way were their opponents flummoxed, for they knew the play to come, yet, could not anticipate the manner of its unfolding and so could not stop the sweep, the dive or the pass.

34 Now, by this encouragement of initiative did the players become their own coaches upon the field, leaving Lombardi no purpose on game day save pacing the sideline and shouting in his easy to hear manner.

35 For Lombardi had taught them well, and thusly did they know him afresh as a teacher, as well as a preacher and a slave driver.

"... Lombardi cast down the false playbook..."

36 Finally, they would know him as a father, for he loved them like unto a family and he said unto them, "Ye are tasked with a test of love, a test of your heart. For it is easy to love perfection but hard to love the imperfect man at thy side."

37 "Now, as ye sacrifice for one another through love, ye will suffer. But without love, ye will find no happiness."

38 "For even lowly geese support one another in their flight of freedom. Are we no less than they?"

39 And so, having the sense God gave geese, the Packers took Lombardi's words to heart and loved one another and stopped plucking each other, placing cooperation above self, affirming Lombardi's claim that, "Teamwork is what the Green Bay Packers are doth about."

40 Thusly did they dwell in the bosom of Lombardi.

41 Thusly did they escape demonic possession and cast away misfortune from their midst.

42 Then did God's ordained retribution end, and He dideth return to His other hobby, cursing the Cubs.

43 And so, The Green Bay Packers followed Lombardi as he led them, soaring across the firmament of football Glory that God had promised unto the faithful.

44 For it seemed the Green Bay Packers, through humility, had received the strength of God, or at least a good second wind.

45 For did not the congregation behold the Green Bay Packers smite all before them, without surcease, those that did not flee before them?

46 "You betcha," said the cheeseheads.

47 And were not the Green Bay Packers a mighty storm of heaven, like unto a great swarm of mosquito, only fewer and much larger?

48 "Dam strait dere," said the cheeseheads.

49 For Lombardi had created a juggernaut, leaving the defeated to gaze upon his mighty works with despair, though the vanquished be valorous also. For did not the worthiness of their opponents amplify the virtue of Packer victories?

50 Was it not the mighty Giants whom they did smite pitifully?

Run to daylight.

51 Was it not the mighty Eagles whom they did humble exceedingly?

52 Was it not the mighty Browns whom they did thrash and have their way with?

53 And was it not the Green Bay Packers who defended the honor of the National Football League against the upstart league of marauding Chiefs and rampant Raiders?

54 Verily, Lombardi's Packers won five Championships in but seven years, a feat unsurpassed by any team, any time, any where upon the face of the earth.

55 And did not the faithful behold a future Hall of Fame army with five future Hall of Famers within the offense and six future Hall of Famers within the defense?

56 Verily, eleven future Hall of Famers, one half the starting twenty two! And it seemed a wonderment unto the congregation, such that their jaws did drop, their mouths agape, and their fair minded hearts uplifted at the unfairness thereof.

57 And yet, were these not the self-same Green Bay Packers who did judge themselves losers in the time before Lombardi had come among them?

58 And did they not gain strength through humility as Lombardi taught them, never resting upon their laurels? For all they perspired, did they not aspire?

59 Verily, the Green Bay Packers did not get too big for their britches.

60 For modesty is the lot of the only team in the nation owned by their fans in the smallest town in the League of National Football.

61 Forsooth, unto the cheeseheads, the size of a Packer's heart doth matter only.

62 Hark! Hear ye not all Sconny rejoicing in the faith of the cheeseheads and the courage of their Champions? Hear ye not cacophonous quacking of migrating geese, clanging of cow bells, and crashing of buck antler and ram horn resounding throughout the land of sky blue waters?

63 Hear ye not its joyous reverberation off the knotty pine paneling of the taverns, and echoing off the towering canyon walls in the Dells?

64 Yea, for verily did the cheeseheads harkened unto God's word for to gain His protection. For they did beware.

65 And behold the congregation multiplying

apace, for their number doth increase across the face of the earth by voluntary association, such that cheeseheads straddle every continent and also islands round about, making for a mighty multitude as God had promised.

66 Perchance thou hast seen them, bowling in their pajamas, grilling burnt offerings of bratwurst, devouring cheese, guzzling beer with gusto and offering selfless tribute to civilized combat, without recompense, for pride of ownership and proof of faith.

67 And wherever ye may find them, ye will behold the cheese upon their heads. For they wear it proudly.

68 Now it came to pass, the heresy of Curly Lambeau was forgiven and his legacy recognized so that, upon his passing, New Stadium was rightly dedicated to the founder of the Green Bay Packers, thusly named Lambeau Field, towering over a quiet, residential neighborhood in tiny TITLETOWN.

69 And it came to pass that, seeing Lombardi's work was done, God took Vince, and there was grief and mourning throughout the land, save for the lone loon who yodeled in celebration that such as Lombardi had lived.

70   And a multitude came from hither and yon
     to pay their respects to this great and
     humble soul. This man who began each day
     in devotion to God and ended his days in
     gratitude for God's many blessings.

71   And so, to honor the triumph of Vince
     Lombardi, his name was given over to
     represent the highest achievement in all of
     sport.

72   Thusly, every year's Champions hoist The
     Vince Lombardi Trophy above their own
     heads in respect for his teaching: that the
     highest pinnacle a champion can attain is
     always, and forever more, under Heaven.

             Amen.

"... under Heaven."

Appendix

GREEN BAY PACKER CHAMPIONSHIPS

1929 1930 1931 1936 1939 1944
1961 1962 1965 1966 1967 1996 2010

GREEN BAY PACKERS
NATIONAL FOOTBALL LEAGUE
HALL OF FAME

Curly Lambeau	Bart Starr
Cal Hubbard	Ray Nitschke
Don Hutson	Herb Adderley
John McNally	Willie Davis
Clarke Hinkle	Jim Ringo
Mike Michalske	Paul Hornung
Arnie Herber	Willie Wood
Walt Kiesling	Ted Hendricks
Emlen Tunnell	Jan Stenerud
Tony Canadeo	Henry Jordan
Len Ford	James Lofton
Jim Taylor	Reggie White
Forrest Gregg	Dave Robinson

Vince Lombardi

Made in the USA
Lexington, KY
02 February 2016